Lawler Education · *Literacy Matters*

Reading for Comprehension

Carol Meadows B.Ed. Cert.Ed.

Reading for Comprehension –

ISBN 978-1-84285-420-4

© 2016 Lawler Education

Lamorna House

Abergele

LL22 8DD

United Kingdom

Lawler Education (GLMP Ltd),

Typesetting by Shed Media

Copyright Notice

Number/General Thinking Series
Introducing Algebra 1: Number Patterns and Sequences
Introducing Algebra 2: Specialising and Generalising
Introducing Algebra 3: Introducing Equations
Introducing Algebra 4: Equations and Graphs

Aussie Tales: Developing Morals and Values in KS2 and KS3/P1-6/S1-3
Teaching Guide
Blubber and Floss
Jimmy and the Blue Bottles
Macca Dacca
Magpie Madness
No Presents for Christmas
Ratbags
Shape Shifters
The Copperhead
The Crossover
The Football

Aber Education Teacher Books
Family Relationships
Bullying and Conflict
Hey Thompson
Self-Esteem and Values
Self-Esteem: a Manual for Mentors
Enhancing Self-Esteem in the adolescent
Grief, illness and Other Issues
Survival Teen Island: The Ultimate survival guided for teenagers

Self-Help
Choose Happiness
The Eat Well Stay Slim Budget Cookbook
Write Yourself Well

English
Creativity through Fiction
Creativity through Non-Fiction

Financial Literacy/Capability
Back to the Black for Primary Schools
Back to the Black for Secondary Schools

www.graham-lawler.com

Contents

Contents	
A Car of Her Own	5
Lions	6
Shopping with Dad	7
Fishing	8
The Corner Shop	9
Fall Out	10
The Cross-Channel Ferry	11
Flight	12
My Future Part-Time Job	13
My Fat Teacher	14
Butterflies	15
The Routemaster	16
My Radio DJ brother	17
Re-Cycling	18
My Birthday Party	19
My Grandma	20
Hairdressing	21
Take Away	22
The Football Match	23
The School Trip	24
Decorating My Bedroom	25
My Toys	26
The School Disco	27
The Christmas Party	28
Easter Eggs	29
Blue Peter	30
The Netball Match	31
Extra-Extra read all about it	32
Stamp Collecting	33
The Canary Islands	34
Puppies	35
Skateboarding	36
Graham's Mercedes	37
Bonnie and Clyde	38
Answers	39–40

Introduction

Who is this resource for?

This set of short stories is designed to provide reading and comprehension material that is appropriate for children who are developing their literacy skills. It has been matched to the Curriculum for Excellence in Scotland, the National Curriucla in Wales, Northern Ireland and England and the National Curriculum in Eire.

How is the resource organised?

The stories have been placed according to a graduation that increases in difficulty. The stories are written with simple, repetitious words that are at first short but then increase in length.
Each story is accompanied with a photo or graphic, and comprehension questions.
This resource is produced in the form of blackline master worksheets.

Rights
A teacher has the right to copy these pages with their own children but may not resell this book or lend it out in any format.

A Car of Her Own

Name_____

My mum wanted a new car. She has been driving her old car for a long time and it was very rusty. Mum looked in the papers to see if there were any garage showroom adverts for a second hand car. Mum asked dad to go with her to look at the car. She liked the look of a brand new red sporty car but it was too expensive. It was a shame because I really liked that one as well. Then mum and dad saw a small plain blue car. Mum and dad both drove it and they liked it. Mum paid for the car. It is not as flash as dad's car but it is perfect for mum to take us to school, for her to go to work and most importantly to take me to football on Saturday mornings.

Questions

1. Which car did Mum like first? _____

2. Circle True or False for each statement.

   True   False   Both mum and dad drove the car.

   True   False   The blue car looked sporty.

   True   False   Dad paid for the car.

   True   False   The red car was second-hand.

   True   False   The blue car was new.

3. Fill in the missing words.

   Mum takes me to _____ on Saturday mornings.

   Mum's old car was covered in a lot of _____.

   Mum has a _____ car.

   My dad helped _____ to look at cars.

   You don't want your car to _____ _____ on the job.

4. Why do you think mum bought the blue car?

   _____

5. Join the matching parts of the story.

   The first car mum looked at   her car to break down.

   Mum   use for work.

   Mum didn't want   cost too much.

   Mum needed a car to   bought the blue car

Lions

Name_____

The lion is part of the cat family. It is related to pet cats we keep in our houses. Lions live mostly in Africa and India. The male lion has a thick mane of fur around his face. He has a tuft at the end of his tail. He has strong, powerful legs. The female lion is called a lioness. She is smaller than the male lion. Her coat is smooth. She has between two and six cubs in each litter. Lions live together in groups called prides. There are usually several members in a pride. One male lion is usually the boss. Lions are carnivores. This means that they eat meat. They have sharp teeth and strong jaws. Their claws are large. They can run very fast. For food, they chase animals and kill them. The whole pride shares the food.

Questions

1. Name three differences between male and female lions.

   _____

   _____

   _____

2. Find these words in the story. Write down words that could replace each one, that means about the same. After you have done this, check your words in the dictionary.

   pride _____

   boss _____

   fur _____

   chase _____

   tuft _____

3. Circle True or False for each statement.

   True   False   Lionesses have only one cub in a litter.

   True   False   The pride is made up of females and cubs.

   True   False   Lions are found all over the world.

   True   False   Lions kill other animals for food.

   True   False   Male and female lions are about the same size.

4. Circle ten words in the story that describe lions.

5. What is the most interesting thing you learned from this story?

   _____

   _____

Shopping with Dad

Name_____

My name is Andrea. I live with my dad in a flat. My mum died when I was a baby. I have chores to do. Dad does not like shopping. But I do. That's why shopping is one of my jobs. First I have to make a list of things to buy. Then I talk it through with dad and he gives me the money. I must keep to budget. I don't just buy food. At times we need loo paper, detergent, cleaner or other things. When I get inside the supermarket I choose a trolley. I look at my list and decide where to go first. Since I shop at the same supermarket each time, I know my way around.

Questions

1. Why does Andrea do the shopping? _____

_____

2. Circle True or False for each statement.

   True   False   Andrea lives with her mum and dad.

   True   False   Andrea has chores to do.

   True   False   Andrea has only food on her shopping list.

   True   False   Dad and Andrea meet to write the list.

   True   False   Andrea enjoys her chore of shopping.

3. Draw a line to match each word with its meaning in the story.

   trolley   chore

   split   things you write down

   job   large shop

   list   shopping cart

   supermarket   share

4. Put a circle around each time the word I is used. How many did you circle? _____

5. List 10 things you might buy at a supermarket.

_____

_____

 _____

_____

_____

_____

Fishing

Fishing is a very popular sport in Europe. Many fishing enthusiasts don't really care if they catch a fish or not. They enjoy sitting peacefully and waiting. It is very calming. Most people use a fishing line or rod. The line usually has a hook on the end. People often use worms for bait. Sometimes nets are used to catch some fish, like whitebait and flounder. Nets do not have hooks. Fishing is not only a sport. Some people earn their living fishing. Commercial fishers have big fishing trawlers with nets or lines. Fishing trawlers go a long way out to sea. Fishermen can spend many days out at sea fishing. They have to keep the fish they have caught cold so that the fish stay fresh. If the fish does not stay fresh it is called spoiled and cannot be sold. When fishing trawlers come back to the dock, their catch is unloaded and sent to a factory. The fish is sent to the shops where we can buy it as fresh fish. Sometimes the fish is canned or dried. Fish is a great food, not just as fish and chips.

Questions

1. Draw a line to match each word with its meaning in the story.

    worm   dock

    rotten   liked by many people

    popular   used for bait

    jetty   spoiled

2. Name two kinds of fish caught in a net. _____   _____

3. Number each sentence to show the order it happened.

    _____ The fish are kept cold.

    _____ The fishing trawler goes a long way out to sea.

    _____ The fish are unloaded.

    _____ The fish are sold.

    _____ The fish are caught.

4. Why do some people go fishing and don't care if they don't catch anything?

    _____

5. Circle True or False for each statement.

    True   False   Fishing nets do not have hooks.

    True   False   Fishing is a job and not a sport.

    True   False   Spoiled fish cannot be sold.

    True   False   On a fishing trawler only nets are used to catch fish.

    True   False   All fishermen send their catch to a factory.

The Corner Shop

Name_____

A corner shop is a small shop. Most towns and villages have a corner shop although these days they are not always on a corner. In a corner shop you can buy all sorts of things. In the corner shop near where I live I can buy milk when we run out at home. I can also buy bread and newspapers at the weekend. Corner shops are usually owned by a family. They don't have as many things as a supermarket. Many people only buy one or two things from a corner shop but would buy a lot more from a supermarket. The supermarket is further away and that means I have to drive my car there. I do buy most of my food from the supermarket. It is easier to get to the corner shop but things are more expensive there than in the supermarket.

Questions

1. Write down three ways that corner shops are different from supermarkets.

   _____

   _____

   _____

2. Fill in the missing words.

   Corner shops are small shops they are usually owner by a _____.

   I buy most of my _____ the supermarket.

   The corner shop is _____ to where I live.

3. The main idea of this story is _____

4. Write other words for these words.

   quick   _____

   both   _____

   home   _____

   supermarket _____

   corner shop _____

5. Write out the words for these prices.

   £10.00 _____

   £15.50 _____

   £2.65 _____

   £5.30 _____

Fall Out

Name_____

My dad used to be a soldier and went to places like Iraq and Afghanistan. He was lucky he did not get shot like some men and women did. Dad did see some people killed. The trouble is when he left the army and came home he would get really angry. If I left the radio on in my room I would get a row. This was a really bad time. Dad was suffering from an illness called Post-Traumatic Stress. Things were so bad that dad would start to shake and then cry like a little baby. Mum took him to the doctor and the doctor sent him to a hospital. The hospital said this was the fall out from him being a soldier. Dad is a lot better now and the rows have stopped but it was scary for a long time.

Questions

1. Where did the storyteller's dad serve as a soldier? _____

2. Circle True or False for each statement.

   True   False   The storyteller left a radio on.

   True   False   Post-traumatic stress is a fun thing.

   True   False   The storyteller's dad went to a hospital.

   True   False   The storyteller's dad was ill.

   True   False   The storyteller's dad got a lot better and is now far happier.

3. Draw a line to match each word with its meaning in the story.

   cry   when people die through another person's actions.

   killed   place to look after ill people

   hospital   frightening

   scary   weep tears

4. How did the storyteller's mum help her husband to get better?

   _____

   _____

5.   Circle all the full-stops in the story.

Underline all capital letters in the story.

The Cross-Channel Ferry

Name_____

The ferry crossing was really rough. We had left Dover in the South of England for Calais in France and mum was a bit scared. So was I. We headed out to sea. The ferry quickly began to dip up and down and side to side. Waves broke over the deck. The ferry was showered in spray.   Most people tried to walk around, but they were tossed around. They bumped into walls, furniture and each other. Then it happened. People began to throw up. I went out on deck into the fresh air. I needed some space.

The salty sea spray came splashing over my face and specs. Waves crashed all round the boat. At least the air was fresh. I gripped the arms of a seat and stayed there for the rest of the trip. I got soaked. By the time we landed, I was so cold my hands were freezing. I thought I would never get warm but at least I didn't get sick.

Questions

1. Why did the storyteller go out to the deck? _____

    _____

2. Fill in the missing words.

    The _____ were soaking the whole ship.

    Most of the passengers got _____.

    The ferry was getting tossed from _____ to side.

    People were _____ into walls.

    The air was _____.

3. Write down all the words that begin with the letters **sp**. Do not repeat any words.

    _____ _____ _____ _____

4. Circle True or False for each statement.

    True   False   It was a warm day.

    True   False   The ferry was getting tossed about.

    True   False   The boat was wet because it was raining.

    True   False   The people sat down.

    True   False   The storyteller enjoyed the crossing.

5. Find words that mean:

    very cold   _____

    throw up   _____

    thrown around   _____

    went around   _____

Flight

Name_____

The best bit about going on holiday to me is the flight. I love aircraft. When I grow up I really want to be a pilot. When we went to Ireland for a short holiday, we went on a small aircraft. I was amazed there was only one hostess and the aircraft was full of business people. Dad said it was common for business people to fly to meetings on aircraft like this. They are called shuttle aircraft and are treated like buses in the sky. In the same way that we catch a bus to say go to school, business people catch a plane to get to a meeting. On the plane I had a cola drink and some chips. Dad said the posh name for chips is French-Fries. I asked him why they were French and not British but none of the grown-ups knew the answer to that question. I think it is a great question though!

Questions

1. Make up another name for this story. _____

2. Find the meaning of these words in the dictionary. Write another word that means the same for each one.

    business_____   shuttle _____   meetings_____

    hostess _____   French-fries _____   aircraft _____

3. Circle True or False for each statement.

    True   False   The storyteller flew to Ireland

    True   False   The storyteller ate sandwiches.

    True   False   The aircraft was full of holiday makers only.

    True   False   The storyteller wants to be a bus-driver in the future.

    True   False   The storyteller thought the question about French-fries was a good one

4. Circle all the words that describe how you think the storyteller felt.

    angry   scared   cool   anxious   jealous   worried

    hurt   tired   happy   clever   sore   relieved

5. Write words in these gaps tell the story.

    The aircraft was full of _____ people.

    I ate _____ during the flight.

    Dad said the posh name for chips is _____ ____.

    We went to _____.

    There was only one _____ on the flight.

My Future Part-Time Job

Name_____

During the week I go to school and get pocket money from my dad. But when I am fourteen dad says I can apply to be a newspaper boy. That will mean getting up really early in the morning. That is ok because I really like the early mornings. Dad says it is important to get used to the idea of working and earning money. I think it is great because I will have my own money and I will be able to save to go to college. I am planning to get into a computer technology course. I love working on computers

My brother is a lazy slob. He will never get up in time for school and so we are often late. It is a real pain because I have to do detention because of him. Brothers who needs them!

Questions

1. What did the storyteller mean when he said his brother was a 'lazy slob'?

    _____

    _____

2. Circle True or False or Didn't Say for each statement.

    True   False   Didn't say   The storyteller wants to be a newspaper boy.

    True   False   Didn't say   The storyteller's brother gets up early.

    True   False   Didn't say   The storyteller likes riding his bike.

3. Draw a line to match each word with its meaning in the story.

    weekend   a school for adults

    college   job that takes some of your time

    part-time job   a note asking for help

    advert   Saturday and Sunday

4. What does the storyteller have to do, because he has a lazy brother?

    _____

5. Fill in the missing words.

    The storyteller can apply to be a paper boy when he is _____.

    The storyteller likes _____ mornings.

    The storyteller really likes the idea of being a _____ boy.

    The storyteller has to do _____ because of his brother.

My Fat Teacher

Name_____

I feel really silly. My teacher is Mrs Jones and she has been off school for a while. When she was in school she had to sit down a lot and rest and she looked really fat. One day I saw her eating lots of biscuits. I thought that is why you look really fat Mrs Jones. My mum told me that eating the wrong kind of foods can be bad for you. Biscuits are a nice treat but Mrs Jones was stuffing them away like crazy and her tummy was huge. I wanted to say something to help her but couldn't think of a nice way to say ' Mrs Jones stop stuffing the biscuits down', so I said nothing. When she was away I thought, ' I hope she is on a diet'. When she came back I was amazed at how much slimmer she was. I said ' Mrs Jones you look great so much slimmer now, see those biscuits are not a good idea are they.' It was my best disapproving voice. Mrs Jones said, 'Maisie I wasn't fat from eating biscuits, I've just had a baby.' That is why I feel silly.

Questions

1   What is the storyteller's name ?_____

2   What is the storyteller's teacher's name ?_____

3   What did Maisie see her teacher eating ?_____

4   What did the teacher have to do a lot when she was in school ?

_____

5   What was the real reason Mrs Jones looked big?

_____

Butterflies

Name_____

Butterflies and moths maybe some of the smallest living things in the world but they are fascinating. They have a complete life cycle. This means there are four different stages. Each stage looks completely different from the other stages. Every stage has a different job in the life of the insect. In the first stage, the egg is tiny and round and usually has fine ribs. The female sticks the egg to leaves, stems and other objects. They usually lay their eggs near caterpillar food. In the second stage, the caterpillar emerges. It is also called a larva. It is long like a worm. There are often stripes down the side. The third stage is called the chrysalis or pupa. This is the stage where the caterpillar tissues are changed into adult insect tissues. The final stage is the adult or imago. It is colourful and a delight to see in gardens. This is the reproductive stage in the life-cycle and where it can move or migrate to another area.

Questions

1. A butterfly or moth has a complete life-cycle. How many stages are there in the life-cycle ?

_____

2. What is the first stage called? _____

3. What is the second stage called ?_____

4. What is the third stage called ?_____

5. What is the fourth stage called ?_____

6. What is the other name for the adult stage ?_____

7. What does migrate mean? _____

8. What is the other name for a chrysalis ?_____

The Routemaster

Name_____

The Routemaster is the name of the famous double-decker London Bus. It was first built in 1954 and the last one was delivered in 1968. It was built with the traditional half cab, front mounted engine and open rear platform. They entered service with London Transport in 1956 and they were finally withdrawn from service in 2005. Some of the old buses do run on holidaymaker routes, these are called heritage routes. Heritage route 9 goes from Olympia to Trafalgar Square. Heritage Route 15 goes from Trafalgar Square to Tower Hill. Many Routemasters were exported for holiday areas and Niagara Double Decker Tours has one at Niagara Falls in Canada.

Questions

1. What is a Routemaster?

   _____

2. What colour are they in London?

   _____

3. Routemasters started in London in 1936.

   True or False?

   _____

4. Routemasters were withdrawn in 2005

   True or False?

   _____

5. Circle Fact or Opinion for each statement

Fact	Opinion	The Routemaster bus was painted red in London.
Fact	Opinion	Red is the best colour for any vehicle.
Fact	Opinion	Niagara Falls in Canada has a company with a Routemaster.
Fact	Opinion	Heritage Routes are a fun way to ride on an old bus.

My Radio DJ Brother

Name_____

My older brother loves pop music. He is sixteen He has decided he wants to be a radio dj. He says playing records and chatting on the radio is the best job you could get. To start his career, my brother has started broadcasting his radio show on our local hospital radio. Most of his listeners in hospital are older people who are ill. This means my brother has had to study music. He needs to know the music that was popular when his listeners were young. He has to know about old fashioned pop-groups from the 1960's and 1970's, like the Beatles and Abba. The Beatles were really famous in the 1960's and Abba were famous in the 1970's and 80's. Both pop-groups wrote and performed their own songs. That is what made them special. The songs were so good that even now, all these years later, they can still be heard on the radio. My brother likes playing songs like *Twist and Shout* by the Beatles and *The Winner Takes it all* by Abba.

Questions

1. Circle True or False for each statement.

   True   False   The storyteller's brother likes pop music.

   True   False   The storyteller's brother wants to work in television.

   True   False   The storyteller's brother is a radio disc jockey on hospital radio.

   True   False   He has studied old pop-groups like the Beatles and Abba

   True   False   *The Winner Takes it All* was a hit song from Abba.

2. Why does the brother need to learn about old pop-groups ?

   _____

3. Circle Fact or Opinion for each statement

   Fact   Opinion   The storyteller's brother is a hospital radio disc jockey.

   Fact   Opinion   Abba made great songs.

   Fact   Opinion   Most of his listeners to his hospital radio programme are older people

   Fact   Opinion   *Twist and Shout* is a fantastic song.

   Fact   Opinion   Both Abba and the Beatles wrote and performed their own songs.

Recycling

Recycling means using things again. So for instance old glass bottles can be melted down and used again as new glass bottles. This saves money for the companies and means we don't have to throw old bottles into the town tip. So we are not throwing loads of rubbish into the ground for people in the future to clean up. This is called 'Being 'Green' and means we are protecting the earth. This is called 'being kind to the planet.' In our house we have three boxes , a red, blue and green box. The green box is for old food or garden weeds. These are things that will rot down. When they have rotted down they form compost. The compost is like new soil and can be put back on gardens and farmers' fields. This means it is a really good thing to do. The blue box is for old clothes. These clothes can be used as insulation in cars. The red box is for batteries and things that cannot be re-used. Parts of the batteries can be re-used. batteries have expensive metals in them and those metals can be stripped out.

Questions

1. What do recyclers do with old glass bottles?

_____

2. What does 'Being 'Green' mean ?

_____

3. Why are there different coloured boxes ?

_____

4. What happens to old food or gaden weeds that are rotted down ?

_____

5. Fill in the gaps here.

Today most areas recycle. Recycling means _____. 'Being 'Green' means _____. In our house we have three recycling boxes, they are _____, _____, and _____ in colour. Old food and garden weeds make great _____ when rotted down and can then be put back on the garden or the farmer's field. Recycling means we are protecting our planet for the future. It means we will not leave a mess for the people of the _____ to clean up, when we are all gone.

My Birthday Party

Name_____

For my birthday this year my mum gave us a real treat. Instead of having a party at home we were taken swimming. It was brilliant. We had a game of water football. We were in the deep end. My friend Sanjay was in goal. He was not a good swimmer so when the other side attacked he only had one hand to defend the goal. The other hand was hanging onto the side of the swimming pool. He was frightened of sinking. We did not know this before the game. He said he would be in goal because he was frightened of being in the deep end. We lost the game five-nil. Sanjay is still my mate though and it was a brilliant birthday treat, thanks Mum!

Questions

1. What is the storyteller's special birthday treat ?

_____

2. What position did Sanjay play ?

_____

3. Why did Sanjay hold on to the side with one hand ?

_____

4. True   False   Sanjay was a good swimmer.

   True   False   The game was water football.

   True   False   The score was seven-nil.

   True   False   The storyteller's mum took all the people swimming.

_____

5.   Fill in the missing words.

   The storyteller and friends went swimming for a _____ treat.

   Sanjay was a _____ swimmer.

   Sanjay was our _____ for the game.

   It was a brilliant _____ treat for the storyteller.

_____

My Grandma

Name_____

I love going to see my grandma. She is my mum's mum. My other grandma, my dad's mum died before I was born, so I never knew her. My grandma is Welsh. She was born in North Wales. She moved to our area a long time ago for a job. Then she met grandad and they got married. It was a long time ago, in the 1970's. My mum was born in the 1980's. Gran used to be a teacher before she retired. My mum is also a teacher but not at my school, thank goodness. Last week when I went to see gran, with my mum, we had a special treat. When we visited she had cooked Welsh cakes. These are small cakes like pancakes and they are scrummy. When I grow up, I want to be a teacher so I will be the third woman teacher in our family, cool huh!

Questions

1. Where does the storyteller's grandma come from ?

_____

2. What job did her grandma do before she retired ?

_____

3. Why does the storyteller only have one grandma ?

_____

4. When did the storyteller's grandma get married ?

_____

5. When was the storyteller's mum born ?

_____

6. What job does the storyteller want to do when she leaves school ?

_____

7. What are the cakes they had as a treat called ?

_____

8. True   False   The storyteller's mum is a teacher at her school.

   True   False   The storyteller is a girl.

   True   False   The storyteller's grandma was a nurse.

Hairdressing

Name_____

My mum took me to the hairdresser to have my hair done by a stylist. It was so exciting. I have always had long hair. The stylist said I should have a bob. My brother didn't know what that means in women's hairdressing. The stylist cut my hair and washed and dried it. I then had a blow wave. Then I had some mousse on my hair. Hair mousse is great. Hair mousse gives the hair volume. That means it makes the hair look bigger. It also gives the hair a really nice shine. When the stylist had finished my hair, she worked on my nails. I have nice nails. I look after my nails. Every week I put nail varnish on my nails to look after them. The stylist put really cool designs on my nails. One of the designs was stars that sparkled. It was really funky. It was so nice to be treated like a lady.

Questions

1. What word has the storyteller used to mean hairdresser in the first line ?

_____

2. What style of haircut did she have ?

_____

3. What happened after her hair had been washed and dried ?

_____

4. What was put on her hair ?

_____

5. What design was put on her nails ?

_____

6. True   False   The storyteller had a bob style haircut.

   True   False   She had her hair dyed red.

   True   False   One of her nail designs was stars that sparkled.

Take Away

Name_____

My dad is so cool. On a Thursday night mum goes out to keep fit and dad is left to cook our dinner. So we wait until mum has gone and then we go out in the car to a burger bar. It is brilliant we get to eat fries and burgers once a week as long as we don't tell mum. Last week I had an extra size burger and a cola. Dad doesn't have anything because he says he doesn't like burgers. I don't know what is wrong with him. My sister used to enjoy it but says she doesn't like it as much now. She says she cannot get her best top on anymore. My football kit is a bit tight as well. Afterwards when we get home I feel stuffed but can always manage a slice of toast before bed. I wonder why my football kit is getting too tight!

Questions

1. What night did their dad take the storyteller and his sister out ?

_____

2. Why do they go out on this night ?

_____

3. What did the storyteller have to eat last week ?

_____

4. Why do you think his sister doesn't like going as much ?

_____

5. Why do you think the storyteller's football kit is getting too tight to wear ?

_____

6. Draw a line to each half of the sentence.

Mum goes out	tell mum we go out to the burger bar.
Dad takes us	to keep fit on a Thursday evening.
My sister can't	getting to tight to wear.
My football kit is	to the burger bar when mum is out.
Dad said we must not	wear her best top anymore.

The Football Match

Name_____

The game was not going well. We were two-nil down and we had already had one player taken off injured. The P.E. Teacher Mr Salter shouted, 'Morrison you're on'. Graham Morrison came on as a defender and then everything changed. Graham Morrison played a blinder, he took a long ball across the pitch near the half way line. I could not believe what I saw then. He just let fly from the half-way line with a huge strike and stood. The ball flew across the pitch and straight into the top corner of the goal. Now it was 2-1 and we were back in the game. They kicked off from the centre and were on the attack. Morrison tackled their attacker and went passed another player then he squared the ball in the centre. Jones took the pass and hammered it home. In three minutes we had turned the game around. Now it was 2-2. Then after about six minutes we were attacking and there was a goal mouth scramble. The ball was saved off the line and bounced out but Morrison had seen it coming and he thundered it home. we won 3-2. What a brilliant game and well done Graham Morrison.

Questions

1. Why did the teacher make a substitution ?

_____

2. What was the name of the substitute ?

_____

3. Describe how Morrison scored his first goal.

_____

_____

4. Describe what happened to score the second goal.

_____

_____

5. How did Morrison score the final goal ?

_____

_____

The School Trip

Name_____

The school trip had been planned for weeks. We did a lot of work about North Wales, where we live, in our geography class. Now the big day had arrived. We were going to Snowden, the highest mountain in Wales. When we got there we were able to ride the railway to the top of Snowden. It was a fantastic day. We went there on a coach and we sang songs all the way. Mrs Richards led the singing and it was a great laugh. When we got there we were allowed to get sweets from the shop. Then we got on board the train and I loved it. The train took us right to the top of the mountain. At the top there is a new cafe where we had tea and our sandwiches. I took photos of the old train on my phone and emailed them home to my mum. She emailed back to say they were brilliant. Thanks Mrs Richards it was a great day out.

Questions

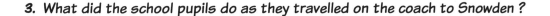

1. Where is Snowden ?

   _____

2. Where does the storyteller live ?

   _____

3. What did the school pupils do as they travelled on the coach to Snowden ?

   _____

4. Which teacher organised the trip ?

   _____

5. What did they travel on to to get to the top of the mountain.

   _____

6. True   False   The storyteller took photos and emails them home.

   True   False   All the pupils walked to the top of the mountain.

   True   False   The storyteller hated the trip in the train.

   True   False   There is a new cafe at the top of Snowden.

25

Decorating my Bedroom

Name_____

I was so excited. My mum said that now I was older it was time I took some responsibility. I asked her what she meant. She said we have to decorate the house and that means your room as well. So I get to choose the furnishings that go into my bedroom. I don't really like pink girly things that some girls my age like but I do like white and shades of white. So I have decided I wanted a nice warm colour. This is meant to be relaxing and that is what I want in my bedroom. I also want the door painted bright orange. I love orange. I bet my mum won't agree to that one. My curtains are going to be chucked out and I will have a nice draw down blind. Now I will let you into a secret. Mum doesn't know yet but when my bedroom is finished well I will need a new set of clothes. well a girl has to look good to feel good doesn't she!

Questions

1. Why is the storyteller so excited ?

_____

2. What does the word 'decorate' mean ?

_____

3. True   False   The storyteller likes pink 'girly' things in her room.

    True   False   The storyteller likes white and nice warm shades of white.

    True   False   The storyteller wants a nice warm colour in her bedroom.

    True   False   The storyteller wants pink curtains in her bedroom.

_____

4. Do you like the idea of the door being painted orange ? Give a reason for your answer.

_____

My Toys

Name_____

I couldn't believe it. My mum must have lost her mind, or so I thought at first. I was in the loft getting the suitcases down to pack for going on holiday. That was when I found it. By it I mean the box. It was stuffed full of my old toys from when I was little. I was amazed when I found them. What on earth was mum keeping them for? I was also surprised when she said, 'memories'. It seems that every time she sees one of my old toys she gets a little misty eyed and remembers when I was little. It gave me a lot of memories too. I had a wooden farm when I was little and I had loads of fun playing it with it. It had sheep and cows and a little farm tractor and I was thrilled when I found it in the box. I told mum I am too old to play with it now but maybe when I am older, if I have a son then perhaps he would like to play with it when he is a little one.

Questions

1. What did the storyteller find in the box?

_____

2. What did the storyteller's mum mean by 'memories,?

_____

3. What toy did the storyteller have when he was little that brought back memories?

_____

4. What does the storyteller hope will happen in the future if he has a son?

_____

5. What was your favourite toy when you were little?

_____

_____

_____

_____

The School Disco

Name_____

When Mr Ellis the head gave us permission to run a school disco I was really chuffed. I was allowed to be the music producer. That meant I got to choose the cd's that would be played at the disco. To do this I went online and looked at the top forty on both the BBC and independent radio. Then I had to do some maths. A song lasts for about 3 minutes so we could play about 20 songs in an hour. This is because 20 x 3 = 60. So for a two hour disco I had to pick 40 songs. Mr Johnson, our class teacher, said that I had to remember certain things. I had to have some oldies for the teachers; well some of them really are oldies. I then had to remember that at the end of the disco I had to have some romantic songs, so people could smooch, yuk! Anyway I made sure that most of the songs were from today's chart and most of my class loved it. We had the school hall booked and they put colour filters on the lights it was so cool. OK confession time, I did get to smooch with Becky Jenkins, she is really pretty.

Questions

1. List the different types of music mentioned in the story.

_____

2. Who were the two teachers mentioned in the story ?

_____

3. Fill in the missing words

Most of the music was from the _____ forty charts on _____ and independent radio.

We could play about _____ songs in an hour.

So for a two hour disco I need about _____ songs.

_____

4. What did the storyteller do with Becky Jenkins ?

_____

5. How old are the people involved?_____

The Christmas Party

Name_____

The end of term was Wednesday last year, a very odd day to end for Christmas so we had the Christmas party at school on the Tuesday evening. It was a great way to end school. We finished lessons at 12:30 and then all went into the hall. Mr Ashworth, our head, put some CD's on and we had pop music and then we had a video. The video was a film about a group of kids who made a raft and sailed down a river. It looked great fun but Mr Ashworth warned us against doing it and he was right, it is very easy to drown. The gang in the video then spied on their teacher hiding something in the woods. It turned out to be stolen jewels. They had a teacher who was a crook. The video had a scary bit where a bad man grabbed one of the girls from behind and most of the girls on our table screamed but me and my mates just laughed. It was brilliant!

The meal was roast potatoes, with turkey, sprouts and gravy. Most of my mates hate sprouts but I love them. so they all gave theirs to me. Mrs Johnson our class teacher said 'Richard Parks you are being greedy', but I didn't care, after all it was Christmas!

Questions

1 Why was the end of term an odd day ?

_____

2. What happened at 12:30 ?

_____

3. Who is Mr Ashworth ?

_____

4. What did the teacher in the video do ?

_____

5.   Why did Mrs Johnson call Richard a greedy boy ?

_____

6. Do you like sprouts ?

_____

Easter Eggs

Name_____

Easter eggs are special eggs that people give to each other to celebrate easter or springtime. In the Christian religion they are a symbol for the empty tomb of Jesus. Some people think this comes from days when dead people were put into caves and big rocks were laid across the entrance to the cave. These big rocks can look like eggs. The idea of decorating eggs is ancient. Decorated ostrich eggs have been found in graves from 5000 years ago. The modern custom is to have eggs made of chocolate. Some grown ups hide the eggs and the children have to find them on Easter Sunday morning. The grown ups pretend that the eggs were left by the Easter Bunny. It is a lot of fun. When the hunt is over, prizes are often given to the person with the most eggs. Blind children could never play this game so a scientist has developed a beeping egg so that they can hear wheer the egg is hidden. This means they can, for the first time ever, be part of the Easter hunt.

Questions

1. What does the word symbol mean ? (use a dictionary)

_____

2. What type of eggs have been found from 5000 years ago ?

_____

3. What game do some people play on Easter Sunday morning ?

_____

4. How do they decide who has won the Easter egg hunt ?

_____

5. What have scientists done to help blind children join in the fun ?

_____

6. What type of eggs do we have for Easter today ?

_____

Blue Peter

Name_____

You might be surprised to find out that *Blue Peter* is the longest running children's tv programme in the world. It first began in 1958 on the BBC. In those days there was only one BBC channel. It is now on the CBBC channel. The programme format is a magazine/entertainment show for children and it has presenter challenges. These are where the presenters are challenged to do something amazing like canoe down a river for hundreds of miles. During the history of the programme there have been many presenters usually two women and two men at a time. There is also the outside area known as the *Blue Peter Garden*. Lots of outside broadcasts come from the garden and when it is fine they do activities in the garden. The name *Blue Peter* is based on a maritime signal. A flag called the *Blue Peter* is run up. It means the vessel is about to leave.

Questions

1. When did *Blue Peter* first begin ?

_____

2. What is the programme format ?

_____

3. What is a presenter challenge ?

_____

4. Fill in the missing words

Blue Peter began in _____

Blue Peter is the world's _____ children's tv show.

In those early days there was only _____ BBC channel.

The outside area is known as _____

_____

5. Write down the names of the current Blue Peter Presenters.

_____

The Netball Match

Name_____

Netball is a ball sport played by two teams of seven players. It came from early versions of basketball and began in the U.K. in the 1890's. By the 1960's international rules had been made and from 2011 sixty countries had national netball teams. The game is played on a rectangular court with raised goal rings at each end. The game works by each time trying to score goals by passing the ball down the court and shooting it through the ring. Players have positions which give them their name in the team. In general, during the game, a player can hold onto the ball for 3 seconds before passing or shooting. The winning team is the one that scores most goals. The game is very exciting. Most young women see it as a great way to stay fit, healthy and attractive and many carry on playing when they have left school.

Questions

1. True   False   A netball team has 7 players.

   True   False   Ninety countries now have international teams.

   True   False   The game is played on a rectangular court.

_____

2. Fill in the missing words

   Netball is a _____ sport.

   It came from early basketball and began in the U.K. in the _____.

   By the _____ international rules had been made.

_____

3. Most young women see it as a great way to stay fit, healthy and attractive.

   What does ' fit, healthy and attractive' mean ?

_____

_____

_____

Extra-Extra read all about it

Name_____

In the early part of the 20th Century the internet had not yet been invented. There were radio stations but not that many of them and most people could not afford a television. This meant that the main source of news was from the newspaper. In those days newspapers actually did carry news rather than showbiz gossip. To make a newspaper, they have to print it the night before and then ship it in trucks to the newspaper shops where we buy the newspapers. If a news story broke during the day, then it had to wait until tomorrow for the next paper. In really serious cases, where a newspaper had a story that could not wait, they produced another paper that day. This had less pages and was called the 'extra.' When the news stands started selling the extra they would shout ' extra-extra read all about it.' This became a warning that some important news had broken that day. This then helped to sell the extra.

Questions

1. Why were these papers called the extra ?

_____

2. Why did people need an extra ?

_____

3. True   False   In those days newspapers were full of news not just showbiz gossip.

   True   False   Extras were full of fun silly stories to make you laugh.

   True   False   The newspaper boys used to shout ' Extra-Extra read all about it.'

_____

4

Match the start and end of these sentences

An extra was a way of   'extra, extra read all about it'.

The internet had not   getting important news out fast.

The famous shout was   yet been invented and no-one had tv.

_____

Stamp Collecting

Name_____

Stamp collecting is part of the wider study of stamps known as philately. A philatelist may, but does not always, collect stamps. Many people use the term philatelist wrongly. It is wrong to say all stamp collectors are philatelists. Many people collect stamps because they enjoy it, they find it fun. Postage stamps are often collected for their historical value or because they have links to areas of the world that are interesting. Stamp collectors are very important for the people who make stamps. Sometimes the makers produce a series of stamps just for collectors. This makes the value very high and means the countries that make them can earn a lot of money. The first stamp was called the Penny Black in 1840. It had a young Queen Victoria on the front. It was made without the usual stamp perforations and so had to be cut from a sheet with scissors. Unused Penny Blacks are very rare and can be worth a lot of money. But be aware that many companies now make copies of Penny Blacks so you could be conned out of your money.

Questions

1 What is the study of stamps called ?

_____

2. What is a philatelist ?

_____

3. Why do people collect stamps ?

_____

4. What was the first British stamp called ?

_____

5. What is a stamp perforation?

_____

6. Why do you need to be careful when buying a Penny Black ?

_____

The Canary Islands

Name_____

The Canary Islands are a group of islands off the North Africa coast. They are a favourite holiday destination for many British people. Some people think that the name must refer to lots of Canarys but this is wrong. The islands were originally islands of wild dogs. In the old language of Latin, dog is canis and this word gives us canine. This means that the original name of Islas de Canaris really means Islands of dogs. The most populated island is Tenerife. There are 865 000 people living on this island. Many of them are British. One of the main industries is tourism but there is not a lot of other work available. Many young people are now leaving Tenerife and the other islands. A lot of them are going to Scandinavia to get jobs. The main town in the north of Tenerife is Puerto De La Cruz. This is a lovely town but it is mostly for older people. The beach there is a lava beach so it is black. Young people like to go to the south of the island where there are golden beaches and lots of discos to go to.

Questions

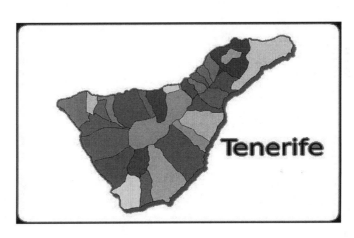

Tenerife

1. Where does the name Canary Islands come from ?

_____

2. What is the Latin word for dog ?

_____

3. True   False   There are 500 000 people on Tenerife

   True   False   Many people who live on Tenerife are British.

   True   False   Many young people leave Tenerife to go to Ireland for jobs.

   True   False   The beach at Puerto de La Cruz is black because it is made from lava

_____

Puppies

A puppy is a young dog. All healthy puppies grow quickly after birth. It is very common for the coat colour of a puppy to change as it grows. Puppy always refers to dogs but a pup can also mean other mammals like seals or even rats. 'Buying a pup' or 'a pig in a poke 'are old fashioned saying that means you have bought an item that is not what you were led to believe it would be. This was from a time in the middle ages when pork was very expensive. So people would be sold a piglet in a bag or poke. Very often when they got home and took the animal out of the bag it was not a pig but a puppy or kitten. This is why people were said to have ' bought a pup' or bought a 'pig in a poke'. When the truth was revealed it was called ' letting the cat out of the bag'.

Questions

I. Name one other type of animal other than dogs, that have pups.

_____

2. What can often happen to the coat colour of a puppy as it grows ?

_____

3. What does 'pig in a poke' mean ?

_____

4. What does ' letting the cat out of the bag' mean in everyday life ?

_____

5. Have you ever bought a 'pup' meaning bought something that was not as good as promised ?

what did you do ?

_____

_____

_____

Skateboarding

Name_____

Skateboarding probably started in the 1940's and 50's in the United States. We are not sure who made the first board but the first manufactured boards were ordered by a Los Angeles, California surf shop. They were meant to be used by people who surfed the waves but couldn't surf when the waves were poor. By using a skateboard they could surf on land until the surf or the waves were back up. Early skateboarding was originally called 'sidewalk surfing'. Sidewalk is the American word for pavement. Skateboarding had low interest until the 1970's. Then a man called Frank Nasworthy developed a new board made from polyurethane. The improvement in traction and performance was superb. This is what caused the popularity of boarding to increase. There are safety problems with skateboards. Pavement cracks can throw a rider so the best thing is to wear a helmet and knee and elbow pads.

Questions

1. When did skateboarding start ?

_____

2. Who ordered the first manufactured boards ?

_____

3. Why did people want to surf on land ?

_____

4. Join the sentences together by arrows

L.A. is the short hand way of saying   a great hit with skateboarders

early skateboarding was called   Los Angeles.

Frank Nasworthy developed   sidewalk surfing

Nasworthy's board was   a polyurethane board.

_____

5. Name three items that are safety items for safe skateboarding.

_____ _____ _____

Graham's Mercedes

Name_____

Graham runs a book business. He takes a number of the books his business publishes to schools to show teachers. The work you are doing now is from one of those books. He needed a new car so he thought he would get a Mercedes Benz. Graham likes these cars because although they are expensive to run, and he is not wealthy, they are strong cars. Graham says that when you have a lot of books in a car it needs to be strong. Books are very heavy. The fact that they weigh a lot means he bought a diesel engine car. Diesel engines are noisier but they do travel further per litre of diesel than a car of the same size would on petrol. This is a way of saving some money.

Questions

1. What job does Graham do ?

_____

2. Why does Graham like Mercedes Benz cars ?

_____

3. Why does a car need to be strong to carry books ?

_____

4. Why did Graham want a car with a diesel engine ?

_____

5. What books have you read in the last month ? Write the titles in the space below.

© 2016 Lawler Education Reading for Comprehension

Teachers may copy these pages for use in their own school. Rights are not transferable.

38

Answers

A Car of her Own p5

1. red sporty.   2.   TFFFF.   3. Football, rust, blue, mum, breakdown   4. cheaper

5.

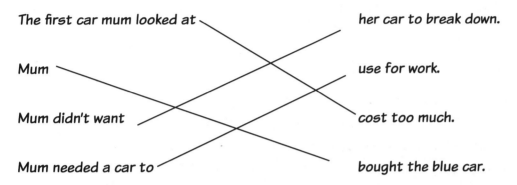

The first car mum looked at — her car to break down.

Mum — use for work.

Mum didn't want — cost too much.

Mum needed a car to — bought the blue car.

Lions p6

1. bigger, thick mane, tuft on tail   2.   pride--- group, boss-----head, fur----coat,

chase---- run after, tuft-----tail.

3. FFFTF

Shopping with Dad

1. She lies it. 2. FTFTT

3.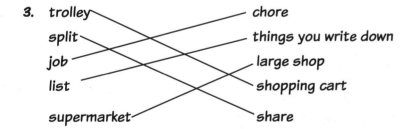

trolley — chore

split — things you write down

job — large shop

list — shopping cart

supermarket — share

4. My name is Andrea. I live with my dad in a flat. My mum died when I was a baby. I have chores to do. Dad does not like shopping. But I do. That's why shopping is one of my jobs. First I have to make a list of things to buy. Then I talk it through with dad and he gives me the money. I must keep to budget. I don't just buy food. At times we need loo paper, detergent, cleaner or other things. When I get inside the supermarket I choose a trolley. I look at my list and decide where to go first. Since I shop at the same supermarket each time, I know my way around.

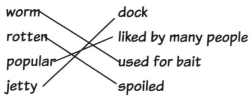

Answers

Fishing

1. Draw a line to match each word with its meaning in the story.

   worm — used for bait

   rotten — spoiled

   popular — liked by many people

   jetty — dock

2. Whitebait, flander

3. Number each sentence to show the order it happened.

   3 The fish are kept cold.

   1 The fishing trawler goes a long way out to sea.

   4 The fish are unloaded.

   5 The fish are sold.

   2 The fish are caught.

4. peaceful and calming   5   TFTFT

The Corner Shop

1. Closer, smaller, owned by family.   2. family, food, closer.

3 To explain the role of a corner shop

4. answers include: fast, 2 or more, place where I live, large shop, small shop.

5 Ten pounds, fifteen pounds fifty pence, two pounds sixty five, five pounds thirty pence.

Fall Out

1 Iraq/Afghanistan.   2. TFTTT.

3. cry — weep tears

    killed — when people die through another person's actions.

    hospital — place to look after ill people

    scary — frightening

4. My dad used to be a soldier and went to places like Iraq and Afghanistan. He was lucky he did not get shot like some men and women did. Dad did see some people killed. The trouble is when he left the army and came home he would get really angry. If I left the radio on in my room I would get a row. This was a really bad time. Dad was suffering from an illness called Post-Traumatic Stress. Things were so bad that dad would start to shake and then cry like a little baby. Mum took him to the doctor and the doctor sent him to a hospital. The hospital said this was the fall out from him being a soldier. Dad is a lot better now and the rows have stopped but it was scary for a long time.

The Cross Channel Ferry

1. Fresh Air, 2. Waves, sick, side, bumped, fresh. 3 spray, space. 4. FTTFF

5. answers include: freezing, vomit, bumped, walk about

Flight

2 answers include: business-companies, shuttle---flight, meetings--- assemblies

hostess----air hostess, French Fries---chips, aircraft----plane.

3 TFFFT   4.   happy, clever.

5. business, chips and cola, French Fries, Ireland, hostess.

My Future Part-Time Job

1. He is idle.   2.   T F Didn't say

3. weekend ⟶ Saturday and Sunday

   college ⟶ job that takes some of your time

   part-time job ⟶ a school for adults

   advert ⟶ a note asking for help

4. Detention   5. 14, early, paper detention.

My Fat Teacher

1.   Maisie   2.   Mrs Jones   3.   biscuits   4   Rest 5   baby

Butterflies

1. 4   2. Egg laying.   3. caterpillar emerging.   4. Chrysalis.   5. adult

6. imago   7. move to another area   8. pupa

Routemaster

1. bus   2. red   3. False   4. true   5. Fact, opinion, fact, opinion

My Radio DJ Brother

1.   TFTTT   2. Older audience   3. Fact, opinion, fact, opinion, fact

Recycling

1. meltdown and reuse   2. kind to the planet 3. to indicate different groups to recycle.

4. compost   5. re-using, being kind to the planet, red, blue, green, compost, future

My Birthday Party

1. going swimming   2. goalkeeper   3. can't swim   4. FTFT

5. birthday, poor, goalkeeper, birthday

My Grandma

1. North Wales   2. teacher   3. other grandma died   4. 1970's   5. 1980's

6. teacher   7. Welsh cakes   8. FTF

Hairdressing

1. stylist   2. bob   3. blow dry   4. mousse   5. sparkly stars

6. TFT

Take Away

1. Thurs   2. Dad took them out   3. extra size burgers   4. getting fatter

5. getting fatter

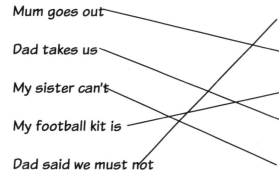

Mum goes out — to the burger bar when mum is out.

Dad takes us — to keep fit on a Thursday evening.

My sister can't — wear her best top anymore.

My football kit is — getting to tight to wear.

Dad said we must not — tell mum we go out to the burger bar.

The Football Match

1. injured player   2. Graham Morrison

3. long shot from 1/2 way line into top corner   4. tackled player, centred the ball

5. rebound.

The School Trip

1. North Wales   2. North Wales   3. singing songs   4. Mrs Richards

5. Train   6. TFFT

Decorating my Bedroom

1. new furnishings   2. apply paint and wallpaper   3. FTTF

4. Student's own answer

My Toys

1. toys   2. memories of her baby   3. farm   4. his own son will play with it

5. student's own answer.

The School Disco

1. Top 40 and oldies   2. Mr Ellis, Mr Johnson   3. top, BBC, 20, 40

4. smooch   5 children/young teens

The Christmas Party

1. Middle of the week   2. went to the hall   3. head   4. hid some jewels

5. he ate a lot of sprouts   6. student's own answer

Easter Eggs

1. a sign   2. Ostrich   3. hunt the eggs   4. most eggs   5. beeper

6. chocolate

Blue Peter

1. 1958   2. magazine/entertainment   3. something tough for the presenter to do

4. 1958, longest, 1, Blue Peter Garden.   5 current presenter names

The Netball Match

1. TFT   2. ball, 1890's, 1960's   3. staying well and looking good.

Extra-Extra read all about it

1. they were extra pages printed that day.   2. no internet/tv   3. TFT

4. An extra was a way of ⟶ getting important news out fast.

    The internet had not ⟶ yet been invented and no-one had tv.

    The famous shout was ⟶ 'extra, extra read all about it'.

Stamp Collecting

1. philately 2 person who studies stamps and everything to do with stamps

3. fun/interest 4. Penny Black 5. paper with holes, to make it easier to tear off

6. lots of fake copies about.

The Canary Islands

1. Islandes de Canaris 2. Canis 3. FTFT

Puppies

1. seals, rats 2 often changes colour, can be darker

3 you have bought something that turns out to be something else that is worth a lot less.

4. revealing the truth, often accidently.

5. Student's own answer.

Skateboarding

1. 1940's/50's 2. LA Surf shop 3. surf was down i.e. there were no waves

4.

L.A. is the short hand way of saying —— a great hit with skateboarders

early skateboarding was called —— Los Angeles.

Frank Nasworthy developed —— sidewalk surfing

Nasworthy's board was —— a polyurethane board.

5. helmet, knee pads, elbow pads

Graham's Mercedes

1. runs a book business 2. strong, can carry a lot of books.

3. books are heavy 4. cheaper to run.